HELEN F

Nocturnes at Nohant

THE DECADE OF CHOPIN AND SAND

BLOODAXE BOOKS

ISBN: 978 1 85224 941 0

First published 2012 by
Bloodaxe Books Ltd,
Highgreen,
Tarset,
Northumberland NE48 1RP.

www.bloodaxebooks.com
For further information about Bloodaxe titles
please visit our website or write to
the above address for a catalogue.

Supported by
**ARTS COUNCIL
ENGLAND**

Cover design: Neil Astley & Pamela Robertson-Pearce.

Printed in Great Britain by
Bell & Bain Limited, Glasgow, Scotland.

CONTENTS

CHARACTERS *7*
SETTING *8*

PART ONE: *Da Capo*

A farewell in winter *10*
The night Sand first heard Chopin improvise *11*
Chopin invites Sand to his apartment *12*
Chopin reflects on the months he and Sand spent in Majorca *13*
A journey in June *14*
Chopin writes to his friend, Julian Fontana *16*
Sand on being at Nohant again *17*
Sand listens to Chopin's Fantaisie in F minor *18*
Delacroix writes in his journal after visiting Nohant *19*
Delacroix's housekeeper complains *20*
The Mazurka – a definition *21*
Sand dances to one of the first mazurkas composed at Nohant *22*
The lovers part for a week *23*
A moment in the life of Tineau, Chopin's valet *24*
Summer in Paris *25*
Chopin on Sand's philosophy *26*
Sand the clairvoyant *27*
Chopin on how the days pass at Nohant *28*
Sand remembers the arrival of Chopin's piano in Majorca *29*

PART TWO: *Ritenuto*

Why a napkin is among Sand's treasures *32*
A night in at Nohant *33*
Delacroix on being an artist *34*
Sand replies to a letter from Delacroix who has just returned to Paris *35*
Ludwika, Chopin's sister, visits Nohant *36*
Chopin writes to his sister *37*
Chopin asks himself one question and answers another *38*

Sand on words and music 39
Sand replies to a question concerning her novel, *The Miller of Angibault* 40
A room of her own 41
Sand regrets inviting another well-known novelist to dinner 42
Sand looks back on her time in Venice 43
A pastime invented by Sand 44
Sand listens to Chopin's Nocturne in E-flat major 45
Chopin on shopping 46
The ghost of Julian Fontana addresses Chopin 47
Sand on her love of the *Vallée-Noire* 48

PART THREE: *Perdendosi*

Chopin's dream 50
Delacroix catches the post-chaise back to Paris after a visit to Nohant 51
Chopin dwells on the past 52
Sand on Chopin's Étude no. 7 in C-sharp minor 53
The Hurdy-gurdy man predicts Chopin's fate 54
Chopin travels alone from Nohant to Paris 55
Delacroix joins Chopin on his afternoon drive 56
One wintry Parisian day 57
These things happened in 1848 58
Solange on Chopin's E minor Prelude 59
The gardener at Nohant remembers Chopin 60
Wojciech Grzymała receives instructions from Chopin 61
The key 62
Solange on Chopin's Fantaisie-Impromptu in C-sharp minor 64
Clésinger permits Madame Sand to view Chopin's death mask 65
Maurice contemplates the manuscript of Chopin's Barcarolle 66
On a winter's afternoon at Montgivray, Solange remembers Chopin 67
Delacroix re-reads a letter received from Sand twenty years earlier 68
Sand, while bathing in the Indre 69

NOTES 70

CHARACTERS

Frédéric Chopin (1810–1849), Polish composer and virtuoso pianist. *Detail from photograph by Louis-Auguste Bisson, 1849.*

George Sand (1804–1876), christened Amantine Aurore Lucile Dupin, novelist. Marriage to Casimir Dudevant in 1822 gave her the title of Baroness. They officially separated in 1836. *Detail from portrait by Auguste Charpentier, 1838.*

Maurice Dudevant-Sand, son of Sand and Casimir Dudevant.

Solange Dudevant-Sand, later Clésinger, daughter of Sand. Probable father: Stéphane de Grandsagne

Auguste Clésinger, sculptor, husband of Solange. Responsible for Chopin's death mask.

Ludwika Chopin, Chopin's sister.

Eugène Delacroix, painter, close friend of Chopin and Sand.

Jenny, Delacroix's housekeeper.

Wojciech Grzymała, friend and confidant of Chopin.

Julian Fontana, studied music with Chopin, copied out many of Chopin's scores.

The **Hurdy-gurdy man**, beggar-musician.

Pierre, gardener at Nohant.

Tineau, Chopin's valet.

SETTING

Chopin and Sand met in the autumn of 1836 in Paris. Just over a decade later their relationship came to an end, but in the intervening years (which were divided between Nohant and Paris), both artists were highly creative. Chopin quickly gave up trying to compose anywhere other than Nohant (Sand's family home in Berry) and many of his greatest compositions were written there. When his connection to Sand and to Nohant came to an end, his creativity dwindled dramatically. Sand continued to live and work at Nohant until her death.

The poems were inspired primarily by Chopin's music and the letters written by both Chopin and Sand. Some poems draw on actual events, others are entirely fictional.

In memory of my parents

With thanks for all the years of piano lessons

PART ONE

Da Capo

Beneath my window, under the screen of linden leaves which covers it, is that window out of which float sounds the whole world would love to hear.

SAND

A farewell in winter

Chopin leaves Poland

I thought counterpoint was all
Elsner could teach me, then
came a lesson in how to part:

use art – compose a cantata,
have it sung in an undistinguished street
just inside the city walls at dusk;

let a head-scarfed figure appear at a door,
let ice crack under wheels,
arrange for a startle of bell-tower birds.

Hold up the carriage, find my face.
The music being performed must say
what speech hadn't and quickly before

Wola's stiff-coated gatekeeper signals
'no more'. Breslau, Dresden, Stuttgart,
then the capital of the world

where, on rainy days, four floors up,
looking out over Montmartre,
I hear still his cantata.

The night Sand first heard Chopin improvise

I was perched on the edge of my seat,
but were the tears that fell
proof of a *coup de foudre*

or of my mother's soul flying in,
freed from the silent winter tree
on which her life got snagged?

Chopin invites Sand to his apartment

Paris, rue de la Chaussée d'Antin

It was winter, very cold.
I was having a soirée,
my oyster-grey rooms
were dusted and swept,
fires lit, ices ordered.
Hothouse flowers spoke
of a climate unknown to me.
Outside, late afternoon light
was meagre, as frost-bitten
as any back-country lane.
I imagined frozen cattle,
liquid eyes fixing me
from across the street.

I close the shutters as guests
begin to arrive; they'll expect
Liszt and I to duet, debate,
Schubert *lieder* and tea.

Seated by the fire, Madame Sand
is quiet, gazes into the flame,
only looks up and listens
when I begin (gone midnight)
to improvise. Before her eyes
a blind brother being buried
beneath a pear tree, a white horse
alone in a field at dusk,
the clamour of a city shut out
by ivy-high walls, the reflection
of a girl in a mirror in Spain.

She invites me to Palma,
calls my excuses lame.

Chopin reflects on the months he and Sand spent in Majorca

That first day as we admired the view,
my hand on the small of her back,
she said the distant glitter on the limpid sea
was like a firework's shower of joy
refusing to dissolve.
                    Of a genie's three wishes,
I'd only need one – that time could be scored
like music! Think of it – two dots to the left
of two vertical lines is all it would require
to repeat the day, or the month, the morning;
for my pen to be again writing 'heaven'
'emerald' 'lapis lazuli' 'dream'.

                    But where is what has been?
I see her turning to me, her hands massaging
the small of her back, at her feet
the buckets of lime our landlord delivered
on my diagnosis as though for swine.

A journey in June

Sand takes Chopin to Nohant

Defeated by Majorca, bored by Marseilles,
here they are on the second day of June
in the heart of the Berry, making their way

along roads lined by chestnut, willows wooing.
Servants are busy laying the oval table
with Porcelaine de Creil, opening doors to rooms –

the freshly hung Chinese red and blue of a chamber
(George has it in mind for Chopin) with its view
over the gardens and all of Berry beyond. A Pleyel

has been installed; he'll have a library, solitude
in which to compose. Le Bois de Bellevue, Montgivray,
the deep, reedy Indre – they're close, cutting through

the back country, watching for the fork at Thevet.
Her motherland, her *terre*, and where her *nom de plume*
must share with 'Aurore', who loves even the names

on the signposts – Sarzay, Châteauroux, Jaunoux.
The lullaby rock of the carriage fails to quiet the waves
of longing rising in its passengers. *I love you,*

Chopin thinks simply but says instead, *Terminée!*
They descend. *Doucement, doucement.*
Children run, dogs wag tails, horses neigh.

George with the gardener – *les rosiers, l'orange doux?*
They dine late, doors open to the terrace,
swifts wheeling, turtle-doves too sleepy to coo.

C'est mon nid ici, thinks George, praying
as she lies awake, loving even the gutters,
that sound she'd forgotten as they fill with rain.

Chopin writes to his friend, Julian Fontana

When the diligence reached the road bordering Nohant,
I promised my angel a waltz and three mazurkas
in as many weeks – Friend, they shall be sent to you
for copying. Is it only a matter of months since Palma,
since I was praising the island's emerald hills, its circle
of lapis lazuli seas, the glorious life I could have sworn
awaited me and my love? But I mustn't return
to that theme. I throw open the windows, breathe.
Visit us (post-chaise to Châteauroux, then La Châtre)
and you shall lack for nothing. The milk is first class.

Sand on being at Nohant again

Here, the distance from my bed to my writing table
is as natural as the distance from my shoulder
to my wrist.
            Discovering that what you're looking for
is at your fingertips – it's like the beauty of rain
seen from a room in which you are at liberty
to remain.

Sand listens to Chopin's Fantaisie in F minor

A few bars and I become Aurore again,
in the gardens at Nohant, little Aurore
with her *grand-mère*. I'm choosing a rose.

Grand-mère will make me a sash to match.
They say we have the same sleepy eyes,
the colour of the Indre where its waters

are in shadow. She stretches out her hand,
my finger tracing its veins as she explains
that rivers always run in search of the sea.

How is it that the Fantaisie which caused
these waves of grief to crash convinces me
I can take more and still be led back to shore?

Delacroix writes in his journal after visiting Nohant

Because my cat Cupid was also invited
I knew my visit would be an oil painting
rather than a sketch, and on the Orléans train
I slept better than I had for weeks.

In the heat of midday Cupid loved to lounge
on the cool cream tiles of the salon floor
and I took to my day-bed with a book.
I'd forgotten life could be so sweet.

George had put a canvas by for a corset.
I nailed it to a stretcher, sent for paints.
And then I was passing the cheese
when I saw exactly how to proceed.

I barely knew my father, and my mother
lost our estates, but when Chopin played
I forgave everyone everything – a result
of the eternal musical principles he obeys?

Delacroix's housekeeper complains

Delacroix painted the garden at Nohant in 1842

What kind of garden requires lead white,
Naples yellow, Vandyke red, green bice,
peach black, Laque Robert no. 8?

Why isn't it enough to be in a garden, to look,
experience and enjoy it? Why does Monsieur
also have to paint it? The doctor ordered rest,

and yet Monsieur writes to request paints,
sends me to Haro's for colours not in his studio,
informs me Pierret will call for wood engravings

and the unfinished drawings he thinks will still be
on the table with the green cloth (as if I wouldn't
have tidied up, given the cloth a good shake).

At least there's logic in vegetable paper
to paint a garden. Find a box in the attic, he says,
and take it to Notre-Dame-des-Victoires.

The Mazurka – a definition

A dance from the Mazur
in which Chopin employed
rubato – a constant
pulse over which some notes
are hurried, others slowed.

Fifty-seven composed
in triple time as though
he knew life would not be
his partner very long.

Sand dances to one of the first mazurkas composed at Nohant

I am mid-twirl, an imagined partner
in my arms, when the music stops.
Dust continues its jig and wine
trembles still in its glass.

I turn to the piano, see your hands
hovering above the keys in the shape
of the final chord as though even you
hadn't seen the end. But every year

when autumn replaces summer,
a book an idea, I'm caught
mid-twirl. And I felt the same
when the woman replaced the girl.

The lovers part for a week

Before leaving for Paris he admired the shimmer
of my gown; its river-green reminded him
of the satiny waters of the Creuse.

Me on foot, he on Margot the donkey,
we'd spent three days exploring the back country
of the river's cut, slipping into deep debate

about the music of the Spheres, his belief
that such a thing exists, but we call it 'silence'.
We lay on the bank listening till the moon swam up.

For me, time had already deposited the trip
in the silt-lands of the past, but for him
we weren't standing on Nohant's doorstep

watching the aimlessness of curled leaves –
no, we were dipping and diving
in a sun-warmed sleeve of the Creuse.

I baptised him with a kiss when he surfaced,
and knew, as the door closed, I'd find the silence
of the next week anything but heavenly.

A moment in the life of Tineau, Chopin's valet

Just hired, he's waiting alone
(as instructed) at 5 rue Tronchet.
The fire is coughing out smoke
when he hears a knock at the door.

As he unfolds Dautremont's delivery
(three pairs of grey winter trousers,
two plain black stuff waistcoats),
a pair of gloves falls to the floor.

In a decade's time, how far will he stretch
the truth when all of Paris follows behind
his old but still young master in his coffin?
Perfect fit, like a second skin.

Summer in Paris

Walking from Rue Tronchet to Pigalle
every day at four
(the hour my Aurore rose)

I never knew I needed Nohant.
But the fact remains: the year
we didn't go, I didn't compose.

Chopin on Sand's philosophy

My dear believes her own dear dead
never departed Nohant; she gathers them
as she gathered semi-perished birds
in 1822, the winter which lives on in talk.

(She used to warm the birds,
Pierre, the gardener, told me,
restore and then free them.)

Nothing is lost ever, she wrote.
Nothing ends once begun.

So, nothingness has no end?

Sand the clairvoyant

A hundred years from now I see ladies
consoled late at night by melancholic mazurkas,
wistful waltzes, their husbands asleep,
their children's eyelids flickering
with dreams.
           Take the new nocturne –
so ahead of its time! I see generations of women
playing over and over the passages
which permit them to confide the most,
tormenting my stupidly jealous ghost.

Chopin on how the days pass at Nohant

The Lady of the House and I fall into our rhythms –
she sleeps in the morning, works through the night,
myself the reverse. Afternoons she rides alone.
Dinner and billiards unite us at five.

My melancholy when it rains is not as acute
as in Paris. Call me a fair-weather composer!
Sunlight settles me at the piano, its warmth
on my back binds my body to the day

(linden leaves at the window, a whiff of smoke,
a dog to stroke), leaving imagination free
to return to the rain, its drench of broken chords,
from which I emerge dry as a bone, ready for tea.

Sand remembers the arrival of Chopin's piano in Majorca

The twenty-four Preludes were completed in a Majorcan monastery

I paid three hundred francs ransom to those pirates
called Customs Officials before they'd release
the Pleyel, then I transported an instrument

with more moveable parts than there were olives
on the trees along five miles of mountain roads
in an unsprung cart.

But hearing the 17th of 24 I crossed out the low notes
in my letter to Charlotte: *Can we complain
of anything whilst our hearts are alive?*

The music made me want to vault higher
than the ceilings, and to congratulate the cloister
and myrtle for living side by side.

What ransom would I not now pay to bring back
our cell, the Pleyel, the closing bars of the 16th
an unsprung spring?

PART TWO

Ritenuto

Our life at Nohant is the same as always...We eat outside: friends come to see us, first one, then the other: we smoke, we chat, and in the evening when they have gone, Chopin plays to me at twilight.

SAND

Why a napkin is among Sand's treasures

When the knowledge was given to me
that time is eternal, I was forty-one.
I continued to shake out my white napkin.

Life is a poem, not a novel. I refuse
such formulae as 'from that moment on'.
If there was an outer sign of inner change

it was not, as you might expect, an augmentation,
rather a reduction: taken away – my ability
in conversation to frame pithy answers;

taken away – the plates from the table
as though the meal could ever be over.

A night in at Nohant

*(One player shuffles a pack of homemade cards, picks a musical key;
the player opposite must describe the key using words or phrases.
Advanced players only: keys can be replaced with single notes.)*

A minor – rain, mansard roofs,
the heart a bedraggled stray animal
looking at the turning of wheels,
the silk button you recall
your mother stitching onto the pleat
of a blue coat with grey lining.

C major – blocks of colour: the sea,
a field, kittens, a child, a daffodil.

E-flat major – white china plates,
to be the last of a party on its way
to the river, the seed-heavy heads
of grasses brushed by skirts, notes
like butter left in a warm dish.

B – on a faded wall of thin-sky blue, the trembling
reflection of the smallest pane in the house,
the late low sun netted in a mesh of leaves.

F-sharp – snow-melt filling the grooves
of carriage wheels as you walk along
rue Rivoli at dusk; the moss which spends
its winter covering the arm of a stone seat;
that woman you remember shaking a red rug
from the first floor window of a white house
in a city you've forgotten or confuse.

Delacroix on being an artist

My skin is lead white,
but I can't rest without working,

can't smell the roses, nor hear
the fountain shake out its water,

nor taste the soil's peach-black
until it exists on canvas.

Sand replies to a letter from Delacroix who has just returned to Paris

My dear friend, has Nohant made you feel
an exile in your own home, duty alone
sending you to climb your studio steps,

submit to the unbearable heat
of rue Furstenberg? My headaches persist;
thank you for the remedy.

You picture us at table, you picture us
on the stone seat by the stream, your easel
you imagine back in the shade of the cedar.

If only we could imitate Cupid, curl up
in the moment! I am in the midst
of what you miss, yet there is part of me

likewise seeing each day from a distance,
an affliction which ether and water
can't cure. In the search for a remedy,

did we stumble across our art?
Thank you for delivering the message
to the gentleman in Place Vendôme.

Ludwika, Chopin's sister, visits Nohant

The door opened. He stood watching me
as I dusted his piano, its polished surface
a mirror in which he held
two steaming cups of *chocolat*.

Meet my brother, a man of such sensitivity
that the shadow of a fly sunning itself
has been known to make him weep.

I seized my chance – by feigning ignorance
of his presence, I relieved him
of the burden of being, and experienced
the power which is his routinely:

who doesn't listen to his music and shine
with relief at the distance
they are given from their lives?

Chopin writes to his sister

Now that you have returned to Warsaw
I confess that once during your visit
I opened the door to my room, found you
dusting the piano with your sleeve.
As though you were a ghost, I froze,
said nothing. You have left behind
your half-embroidered slipper
and a tiny pencil I find most useful.

No matter how beautiful Nohant is,
sometimes I grieve for the emptiness
of space it now occupies for ever.
Observing you while you thought
you were alone – forgive me, but
it was like going back in time.

Chopin asks himself one question and answers another

What can the improvised moments of our lives hope for?
Legato: to be bound together smoothly in a letter?

(*My dearest, 4 o'clock, Sol opens the door*
requesting a duet, embroidery is put down,

picked up, the felling of the frozen tree
is announced, the sun finds a corner to hide)

Or to make their way unannounced into a nocturne, rising
again just when they thought their hiding place secure?

How do I compose? I become a log in the Indre
picking up the floating embroidery of leaves.

Sand on words and music

When I can't write, when I lack
that full feeling I need to propel
my pen across the page and my self
across the day, I request the Prelude
I call my mood medicine.

It's the music to which I'm addicted,
not (as it may appear) the tobacco,
the hookah pipes, sugar water,
Shakespeare (complete).

The Prelude reminds me of the truth
that every living thing must die
and I return to my fiction merciful,
compassionate to the sparkling
as well as to the dull.

Sand replies to a question concerning her novel,
The Miller of Angibault

Am I Rose? Once upon a time
I would have been, but Reader,
you will see from her eye colour
which changes from chapter to chapter,
I regard her as a pretty ribbon
tied round a fête-day bonnet.

Am I Marcelle? Well, we share
aristocratic blood, but mine is mixed
with that of a bird-seller on the banks
of the Seine, so I am both of the people
and not. Marcelle inherits her money,
but by the very act of creating her

(and how many hundred others?)
I will work, shoulder to the wheel,
till the day I die. So am I Grand-Louis,
big-hearted miller, good Samaritan,
but also the fool who rushes in?
You're getting warmer. Now step closer

to the flame. There's the madwoman
coolly burning down her father's house.
She must be somewhere inside me,
just as inside my love of Nohant
there exists the desire to be free,
to be my mother (before me).

A room of her own

Sand remembers her first study

Nohant looks like luxury,
I know, but the only room
which was a dead-end and not
a thoroughfare was far from spacious;
once my books were housed,
my herbs, butterflies, stones,
there was no space for a bed.
A hammock, I thought, and that's where
I slept and from where I leapt
to my secretaire. I overturned the law
which had governed my married life:
rooms with through doors, always
people coming in and out
without cause, traffic, bores.

Sand regrets inviting another well-known novelist to dinner

Balzac came to dinner yesterday,
said he'd discovered a blue rose,
will sell the seeds for fifty centimes.
Chopin's face was a mask
of polite interest, but then,
were he in hell, he'd write music
which smelt of paradise.

I lack his skills – those of an exile
who conquered Paris via its salons,
and thus my face was all impatience
for the plates to be cleared.
I twirled my glass, looked at him,
longing to meet a knowing eye:
Will sales begin whilst blue is still in?

But it was clear Chopin was lost in a room
where blue roses climbed the walls,
where a bunch brightened the piano,
a single petal drifting on the breeze.
*Will the blue be the blue of the roses
in the cheeks of my dead sister?* he asked,
when a flushed Balzac got up to go.

Sand looks back on her time in Venice

I remember the mirror shop, its contents
spilling into the little lost piazza
that one only found when lost oneself.
Framed in gilt, for a moment I saw myself
walking toward myself. It was April.
The starling my lover had given me drank
my ink while I fished for oysters
from canal steps, bought five pence a bottle
Cyprus wine. I wrote letters to my lover
in the presence of my lover and planned
for Constantinople to follow Venice.
Dear young George, what happened?
It's as though you shook my hand,
turned round and walked out of the frame.

A pastime invented by Sand

1 *Sand describes a moment from her past*

My convalescent lover has begun his journey home
and my buoyancy is such I could do without this boat.
Next stop I'll disembark, climb steps, fish in my purse

for the key to rooms which will be mine alone.
I plan to wink at gondoliers, then sleep like a nun.
I'm thirty and I'm free – an orphan, a divorcée.

The entire pride of the city's stone lions roars
as I dip my pen, take aim. From now on
it's my talent I'll nurse for better or worse.

2 *Chopin is required to set the moment to music*

When she described the Venetian memory I knew
first and second clarinets were needed, an insistent
bassoon, oboes, bursts of strings, certainly no legato,
possibly even a trumpet, a bold major key, no drop

to the minor at any point. She needed music
I could never write. This was four years after
she'd said there was no part of her – past, present
or future – which my piano alone did not speak of.

Sand listens to Chopin's Nocturne in E-flat major

Opus 55, no. 2

But this nocturne composed following our scene
(can I not tell any man about a past lover?) –
pure river-light, an altogether unrelated *histoire*,

the proof of its other-worldliness a melody
at once crystal clear and murky, like something
on the tip of your tongue.

It'll be the next mazurka which tells me
where we really stand. I'm guessing
it won't be one to dance to.

Chopin on shopping

Bon Soin soap, patchouli,
bouquet de Chantilly, ivory
head-scratchers, miniature
busts of myself, the choice

of velvet for a waistcoat
(plain black or black
discreetly patterned), gloves
I set the fashion for.

Beware the days when such lists
have no meaning – one's mind
is not on higher things,
but lower (the grave).

That crowd bobbing along
the boulevard below,
they're the ones
on the scent of life.

And if my body allowed,
at the drop of a Dupont hat,
I'd be down there among them,
on the sunny side of posthumous.

The ghost of Julian Fontana addresses Chopin

Concerning my talent, the judgement
of Paris was this: Fontana never rose
above mediocre. Once the city and I
were in agreement, I used a pistol.

So it could be argued, Friend,
that in turning me from fellow student
to unpaid servant you prolonged
my time rather than robbed me of it:

if I was hurrying (*don't dawdle!*)
from the rue des Martyrs to faubourg
St Honoré, thence to your tailor, thence
to your publisher with the scores

I'd laboriously copied out, picking up
your favourite cologne or yet another
pair of gloves, how could I
perform or compose?

My favourite mazurka – of yours?
A minor.

Sand on her love of the Vallée-Noire

It's not just the walnut trees
squaring the paddocks, nor the sight
of Alphonse with his oxen, nor knowing

where to ford the bridgeless Couarde
or Vauvre, nor that the mud in Berry
is superior to that of Paris:

it's the words which only a Berrichon
understands, like *trâine* – too wide
to be a footpath, but with bends

which might prevent a cart from returning
the way it has come, and which might lead
to a swamp or nowhere at all

and whose character (sunken, high-hedged)
means it is a delight at noon
and the haunt of spirits at dusk:

the pleasure of such words is as acute for me
as the pleasure of a return to the tonic chord
for you know who.

PART THREE

Perdendosi

Meanwhile, what has become of my art? And my heart, where have I wasted it? I scarcely remember any more how they sing at home.

CHOPIN

Chopin's dream

On the stage, no concert grand,
no polished Pleyel waiting for my hands.
In its place a beggar-man's *vielle à roue*.
I pick it up, begin to wind out tunes.

(I used to dream in colour, not black and white.)
Looking down, snow half covers my feet.
Beside them, an old tin plate. The audience
stand to leave, throwing a few pence.

The lights go out, a moon rises and still I wind
the beggar's wheel-fiddle, trying to find
a path through the blithely beautiful unfeeling snow.
I wake numb. If she throws me out, where will I go?

Delacroix catches the post-chaise back to Paris after a visit to Nohant

Breaking my journey at Blois further oppressed
rather than lightened my heart –
the château's history of poisonings, plots,
daggers plunged into the breasts of friends.

And despite wide-brimmed memories of Nohant's
white hats, the bourrée's dancing jiggle of colour,
the Vandyke brown of chestnut sauce, for once
I found myself glad of Paris' dusty bustle.

Madame Sand's character Prince Karol – who is this
if not Chopin, and Lucrézia herself – who is this
if not George? Each evening I twisted in my seat
as she read aloud from the novel-in-progress,

Lucrézia's life with the jealous Prince described
as a prison from which she longs to escape.
Even the madder-lake of her voice failed to soothe
my indigestion, for which I blamed chestnuts.

As instructed I delivered Chopin's manuscript
on my first morning in Paris and heard a sonata
in which the cello suggests one topic,
the piano altogether another.

Chopin dwells on the past

Did I love it enough, our life
at rue Pigalle? If I could still compose,
for my inspiration I'd take a corner
of an unpainted picture – her slippers,
the Turkish ones with the toe tassels
I'd tease her for wearing (she'd say
our mattresses were Turkish style,
therefore the slippers). The chewed left foot
permits me to date the picture
to summer 1840, sometime after the day
Mops mistook the slipper for a bone.
How many compositions were ahead,
if only I'd known. Instead, I fretted
that the summer's solitary waltz
would be my last.
                Outside the frame
there's a ladder staircase, our room.
Three vases of Chinese blue hold lilies,
freesias, iris, but open the window,
breathe in the street! We're living
over a carriage-house and stables,
but Lord in heaven, wasn't life sweet?

Sand on Chopin's Étude no. 7 in C-sharp minor

Maurice and I return from our excursion early –
the dwindling autumnal light of the *Vallée-Noire*.

Chopin appears, hanging over him the dug-in mood
of the Étude which I know he will have played

as I like to smoke – lighting the beginning with the end.
No. 7 in C-sharp minor – the pianist required to master

perfect sound and phrasing. Written twelve years ago,
yet the music knows this moment, this day,

how it ends in the hall with our imperfect, half-
uttered phrases, the only welcome sound

Marquis' excited staccato bark, a relationship de-
noted when it's the dog I take in my arms.

The Hurdy-gurdy man predicts Chopin's fate

When she bars her doors against you,
though I stand on the edge of the village
shifting from one foot to the other
in the frost, you'll own me as kin.
Get to know my name – *le Vielleur,*
der Leiermann – all roads are the same
when none lead home. Kick the leaves,
watch the sunset alone, heart sinking.
I'm sorry for you, your consumptive's
dream of Rome. It's further north you'll go,
returning a less-than-seven-stone shadow.

Chopin travels alone from Nohant to Paris

Black Valley rain, plums clotting on the trees,
but she stayed behind to write the last act of her play.

The real-life drama of my journey (the Loire snapping
the bridge at Olivet like a twig, the rope ladder

I clung to swinging twenty feet above a river
the colour of earth) should have warned me.

Instead I acted as though I was still her leading man,
sending parcels of *stracchino*, cloaks of fur,

Madame de Bonne Chose cold cream.
The dearth of letters from Nohant I put down

to a dose of the 'flu and clung to the few
I received as if my life depended on it.

Delacroix joins Chopin on his afternoon drive

Under the carriage wheels, leaves the colour
of Place des Vosges brick in low sun.
We drive through the arch I still think of
as new. The sky-blue eyes of a dog.

What evidence will there be that this day
ever was, that during it a man stood
with outstretched hands while history
(the unseen enemy) was arranging

for the ground-floor room he will die in
to one day be entered by women wishing
to buy face cream? I close my eyes.
Why do I suddenly see the lines

of a chimney pot at Angoulême?
On the Champs Élysées I note the beauty
of a waiter's tray, then our talk turns
to boots, the new shape, a pointed toe.

One wintry Parisian day

The Baroness – Sand's title

My B minor Waltz has been pinched
by the makers of wind-up boxes,
their version the only one I could hear
the day the Baroness sent her boys
to take the billiard table.

I watched it go, its baize grass-green
against the compacted snow
of the square, and I took my cue
to despair.

The last time we met I bowed
once, and then again,
as though I'd been wound.

These things happened in 1848

February twenty-third's drizzle became
the next day's heavy rain. Nothing romantic
about *Paris dans la pluie* as Louis-Philippe
fled, the footsteps of a king echoing
past the heap of men who'd opposed him:
fifty-two dead on rue des Capucines.

At the Square d'Orléans, the composer
opened a letter, then struggled (*forgive
my erasures*) to reply: Solange's child.
Estranged from her daughter and the Pole, Sand
wrote ten thousand rallying words a week
for the *Bulletin de la République*.

But of the barricades, the rioters, the mob,
for an hour or two following her chance
encounter with Chopin (why did she go
to Marliani's?), Sand had nothing to say.
As she watched the man being helped to his carriage,
it faded, History with a capital H.

Solange on Chopin's E minor Prelude

I always play the E minor Prelude
at the grey hour. It has the power
to stow away yet another day I failed

to empty of its promise.
In the scrapbook of memories opened
by the music, this is the one

I turn to repeatedly: I'm ten,
it's raining, we are on an island,
my mother cannot leave without me,

Chopin is teaching me piano,
calls me his little stow-away,
says I'm full of promise (*très bien, très bien!*)

'What's a stow-away?' I ask.
'Something unwanted,' says a voice
I hope every time is not my mother's.

The Gardener at Nohant remembers Chopin

Ravishing, he described my life's work,
and during his seven Nohant summers
I swear my roses grew no longer

towards the ripe Berry sun,
but the window (always thrown open)
out of which his music spilled.

He took the daughter's side, they said.
And that was that.
When Madame was out of earshot

I did my best to hum what I could remember
(a waltz or two and some tunes
that sounded like the words were missing).

Wojciech Grzymała receives instructions from Chopin

As he passed between his sitting room
and bedroom, he wished life
to smell sweet.

Perhaps there'd been an early sweetheart,
the flower's namesake, and it's her
he hoped to summon,

diverting his thoughts from winter, from age,
from the bad smells of the body
as it withers.

Lord, to see him shrinking towards
the little bunch, unable to breathe in
without coughing.

I knew it wouldn't be long
before he passed between this life
and the next.

The key

The verb 'would' – I know how it will be used
to sweeten accounts of that summer,
my twentieth (its musical equivalent
being the key of D-flat major):
On warm summer nights the piano would be wheeled
onto the terrace and Chopin would play
until the light failed, and family and friends
felt their hearts fill to the brim; it was said
even the waters of the nearby Utrata
would slow, listening for longer.

Find the average summer temperature
on the Mazovian plain, put yourself
in my skin – I'm sickly, I'm on a diet
of acorn coffee, tisane, ripe fruit and gruel.
How many nights, then, do you imagine
I'd have been happy for the piano
to exchange the drawing room fireside
for the terrace?
               It did happen, once,
on a soaring midsummer's day when we all
experienced the world an octave higher.
Playing on the terrace, I romanced the river,
I made the willows weep, I stopped mid-leap
wild things in the White forest. I was back
where I was born.
               When I'm dead,
snow making the geese invisible, the only sound
the single plaintive note of the chimney's smoke,
'remember those summers', they'll say.

In my biography, turn a few pages
(not many) and another piano
is being wheeled from an airy drawing room
in Place Vendôme, but this time to a bedside,
darkened. Even then, those long last nights
with Ludwika by my side, if I heard her use
the key of D flat (*we'd go there every summer,*
there'd never be a cloud in the sky)
I refused to let it pass uncorrected.
'Wrong note!' I'd say, having searched
all my life for the key of how it is.

Solange on Chopin's Fantaisie-Impromptu in C-sharp minor

It's when the melody returns but in the left hand
that my eyes fill. Written before we met,
this music tells me I'm intimately known:

someone for whom life never came right –
the daughter not the son, accompaniment
not melody, semitone not tone.

On days of major scenes between my mother
and myself, my face by dinner a scrunched-up
chromatic scale, my brother at the table's head,

Freddy would play the Fantaisie in which rage
is balanced by understanding, today by tomorrow,
and in which the left-out are included.

When he died it was my arms
which held him. The left and the right,
with equal strength they held him.

Clésinger permits Madame Sand to view Chopin's death mask

I didn't know I had a desire
to punish her until she stood
in front of his death mask.

Good, she said, his end was peace.
I'm afraid not, Madame;
all my skill was needed

to compose a mouth so contorted
that his sister smashed
the first mask: she commanded me

to re-do my work, to mould features
which look as though death was no more
than a gentle diminuendo.

Madame looked around the room.
Where are the shattered pieces
of the true mask?

(She was fighting tears) –
If I put them back together
it'll be as if I'd been with him.

Maurice contemplates the manuscript of Chopin's Barcarolle

Barcarolle: originally a Venetian boating song

On my wife's piano, the Barcarolle, the notes
pinned down between five parallel lines
which they either lie between or straddle.

Years ago it was I who said *no* to Venice.
He wrote the Barcarolle anyway, saying,
An artist travels wherever he wishes in his head.

At its first performance, my mother's handkerchief
was dry in her hand while her tears flowed –
I remember the miniature ripples as they dropped

from her chin into her glass of Berry's amber wine
which she said was the colour a thousand waterways turn
when the angle of the sun scatters dome-gold.

Every night the gondola he never rode sails
into my house as my wife plays, her body
tilting, swaying (she's under the Bridge of Sighs,

now at the mouth of the Grand Canal).
Can you be cuckolded by a dead composer
and his city of the imagination?

On a winter's afternoon at Montgivray, Solange remembers Chopin

Because he was always up for checkers
or a ride in the buggy, perhaps I cost him
an extra opus or two, half a dozen
ballades instead of four.

But whenever I knocked on his door,
Sol, he'd smile, putting down his pencil,
turning from his score. For my sake,
the sonata would be stalled

and for an hour or two I had the gall
to delay (and maybe alter?) music
royalty was waiting to applaud.

At turreted Montgivray, growing old
with no one to pass the time of day,
no child, no dog, just the sound
of a burning log, I tried poetry,

but longed for interruption, to see
my young self poking her head
round the door, her *Alors?*

Delacroix re-reads a letter received from Sand twenty years earlier

Dark reflections? she'd written, stride over them!
And if you can't achieve this as yourself,
she went on, then dress up as someone else.

She herself kept the cape of a dead general
for this very purpose: 'With that over my shoulders
I obey every command I give myself!'
Responding, I was dismissive of such tactics.

She'd laugh like an insolent foot soldier
if she could see my wardrobe now –
Iowa Indian, Apollo, an Arab, even a queen!

What a useful strategy it's been, perversely
confirming my true identity: the days
I wear my artist's smock, I am defenceless
against all reflections, dark or otherwise.

Sand, while bathing in the Indre

I even do it in the rain – an acquired taste!
How whole one feels when not just the earth
but the sky too is composed of water.
And without me lifting a finger, as I laze here,
the Indre must be carrying particles of me
to the Loire, the Loire to the sea.
So when I'm obliged to acquire death's taste
it won't be the whole me swallowing.

I'm old, but as an artist I've swum in the past
all my life. And as a woman – as a woman
I've tried to send some of me on ahead.
And women *are* rivers, aren't they?
At least that's what Chopin used to say,
forever slipping through your fingers.

NOTES

Da Capo: a musical instruction to go back again to the beginning of the piece.

A farewell in winter
Józef Elsner: head of the Warsaw Conservatoire and Chopin's teacher. Chopin was twenty when he left Poland, never to return.

Chopin invites Sand to his apartment
Lieder: a term particularly applied to the German romantic songs of Schubert, Schumann, Brahams and others.

Chopin reflects on the months he and Sand spent in Majorca
Along with Sand and her two children, Chopin travelled to Majorca in November 1838. The party spent a difficult winter on the island, during which Chopin was diagnosed with consumption.

A journey in June
Nohant: the manor house Sand inherited from her grandmother, where she spent much of her childhood, and where she eventually died.
Berry: Nohant is situated in Berry, a region located in central France.
Pleyel: Chopin's preferred make of piano.
Terre: ground, but also homeland.
Terminée: finished.
Doucement: gently.
C'est mon nid ici: This is my nest.

Sand listens to Chopin's Fantaisie in F minor
Fantaisie: a movement in no specific form but in improvisatory style.
Grand-mère: Grandmother

Sand the clairvoyant
Nocturne: night-piece, a musical form which Chopin made all his own.

Ritenuto: a musical term meaning 'held back'.

Sand replies to a letter from Delacroix who has just returned to Paris
Cupid: Delacroix's cat.

Chopin asks himself one question and answers another
Legato: a musical term meaning 'smooth'.

Sand looks back on her time in Venice
Prior to meeting Chopin, Sand spent several months in Venice with her lover, the poet Alfred Musset.

Sand listens to Chopin's Nocturne in E-flat major
Chopin's mazurkas have been described as his most personal works in which he 'jotted down all his changes of mood'.

Sand on her love of the *Vallée-Noire*
Vallée-Noire: the Black Valley, a region of the River Indre and its tributaries in Berry.
Berrichon: a native of Berry.

A pastime invented by Sand
My convalescent lover: i.e. Alfred Musset.

Perdendosi: a musical term meaning 'dying away'.

Chopin's dream
Vielle à roue: hurdy-gurdy or wheel-fiddle, a popular instrument in Berry.

Delacroix catches the post-chaise back to Paris after a visit to Nohant
Bourrée: a dance often performed in the square outside Sand's house.
Lucrézia Floriani: novel by Sand published in 1846.

Sand on Chopin's Étude no. 7 in C-sharp minor
Étude: a piece of music designed to give practice in some branch of instrumental technique

The Hurdy-gurdy man predicts Chopin's fate
Veilleur, Leiermann: hurdy-gurdy man.

These things happened in 1848
Paris dans la pluie: Paris in the rain.

The key
Mazovian plain: the plain surrounding Warsaw.

Solange on Chopin's Fantaisie-Impromptu in C-sharp minor
Chromatic scale: a scale in which all the steps are semitones.
Semitone: the smallest distance between two notes on a keyboard.

Clésinger permits Madame Sand to view Chopin's death mask
Diminuendo: a musical term for diminishing the tone, getting softer.

Maurice contemplates the manuscript of Chopin's Barcarolle
Sand's plan to winter in Venice rather than Paris for the sake of Chopin's health was opposed by her son, Maurice.

On a winter's afternoon at Montgivray, Solange remembers Chopin
Alors: well, so.

ACKNOWLEDGEMENT

This collection owes its existence to an edition of BBC Radio 3's 'Composer of the Week' which focused on Chopin's time at Nohant, and to a timely sabbatical granted by the English Department at Lancaster University.